The TRUTH ABOUT OGRES

BY ERIC BRAUN

ILLUSTRATED BY SHAWNA J.C. TENNEY

KEEP OUT!

PICTURE WINDOW BOOKS
a capstone imprint

Thanks to our advisers for their expertise, research, and advice:

Elizabeth Tucker, PhD, Professor of English
Binghamton University, Binghamton, New York

Terry Flaherty, PhD, Professor of English
Minnesota State University, Mankato

Editor: Shelly Lyons
Designer: Lori Bye
Production Specialist: Michelle Biedscheid
Art Director: Nathan Gassman
The illustrations in this book were created digitally.

Picture Window Books
151 Good Counsel Drive
P.O. Box 669
Mankato, MN 56002-0669
877-845-8392
www.capstonepub.com

All books published by Picture Window Books
are manufactured with paper containing at least
10 percent post-consumer waste.

Library of Congress Cataloging-in-Publication Data
Braun, Eric, 1971-
The truth about ogres / by Eric Braun, illustrated by Shawna J.C.
Tenney.
p. cm. — (Fairy-tale superstars)
Includes index.
ISBN 978-1-4048-6159-6 (library binding)
1. Ghouls and ogres. I. Tenney, Shawna J. C. ill. II. Title.
GR560.B66 2011
398.21—dc22   2010026900

Printed in the United States of America in North Mankato, Minnesota.
092010   005933CGS11

Are Ogres Real?

Have you ever heard stories about nasty creatures called ogres? Maybe you've wondered if ogres are real. Don't worry! Ogres are pretend monsters in fairy tales.

What Do Ogres Look Like?

Ogres are a kind of giant. They look like really big people. They have strong bodies, lots of hair, and a beard. Their heads are usually too big for their bodies. Most ogres have big mouths with large teeth. Because ogres eat a lot, they often have round bellies. They also smell horrible.

big heads
full of hair

big mouth

beard

large teeth

strong body

round bellies

5

Ogre Behavior

Most fairy-tale ogres are mean and powerful. But they are not very smart. That's lucky for the people who find them! A person can easily trick an ogre.

A female ogre is called an ogress. Ogresses are not as mean as male ogres. In stories, ogresses sometimes end up helping people.

Ogres are different from other giants. That's because ogres like to eat people. They often steal children or princesses. But many times, people outsmart ogres.

In the Russian tale *The Children on the Pillar*, children and their animal friends trick an ogre. The ogre's magical bone hurts the ogre instead of a boy.

In the Italian tale *The Ogre's Breath*, an ogre steals a princess. He keeps her in a castle and hopes to marry her. But seven brothers work together. They save the princess from the ogre.

Some ogres have magical powers. The ogre in *Puss in Boots* can change into other animals. A cat tricks the ogre into becoming a mouse and eats it. Then the cat and his master take over the ogre's riches and castle.

Where Do Ogres Live?

In most stories, ogres live deep in forests or on mountains. Some ogres live in caves. Others live in castle dungeons.

Most ogres like to live alone. Sometimes they guard treasure. If people get too close, the ogres might attack.

14

History of Ogres

Stories about ogres have been around for hundreds of years. The ogre legends come from all around the world. Many of the tales were spoken before they were written down. Authors from Italy and France wrote some of the first ogre stories.

The Flea is a story in a collection of tales from 1634. It is one of the first written stories to include an ogre. In the story, a king keeps a flea. It grows to the size of a sheep! The king asks people to guess what the animal is. An ugly ogre guesses correctly. As a prize, the ogre gets to marry the beautiful princess.

Ogre Stories

Ogre stories became common after 1697, when Charles Perrault's *Tales of Mother Goose* came out. Some of the tales from this book had ogres or ogresses in them.

In *The Sleeping Beauty in the Wood*, an evil ogress wants to eat her son's wife and kids. But she is outsmarted by a servant who gives her lamb meat instead. When the ogress figures out the trick, she throws herself into a pit of snakes.

Another story from *Tales of Mother Goose* is *Little Tom Thumb*. It's about Tom Thumb, who is the size of a person's thumb. Tom and his brothers escape being eaten by an evil ogre. Later they trick the ogre's wife into giving them riches.

Jack and the Beanstalk is a famous ogre tale. The story tells of a young boy named Jack. He climbs a tall beanstalk into the clouds. There he finds an ogre's castle filled with treasure. Jack steals some of the treasure. The hungry ogre chases him down the beanstalk. On the ground, Jack chops down the beanstalk. The ogre falls to the earth.

Ogres Today

Stories of ogres are still popular today. The book *Shrek!*, by William Steig, was made into a series of movies. The book is about an ogre named Shrek who leaves his swamp home. With the help of a donkey, Shrek finds an ogress princess and falls in love with her.

Ogres show up in many of today's stories. *The Chronicles of Narnia* series by C. S. Lewis features ogres. They also show up in *The Spiderwick Chronicles* series by Tony DiTerlizzi.

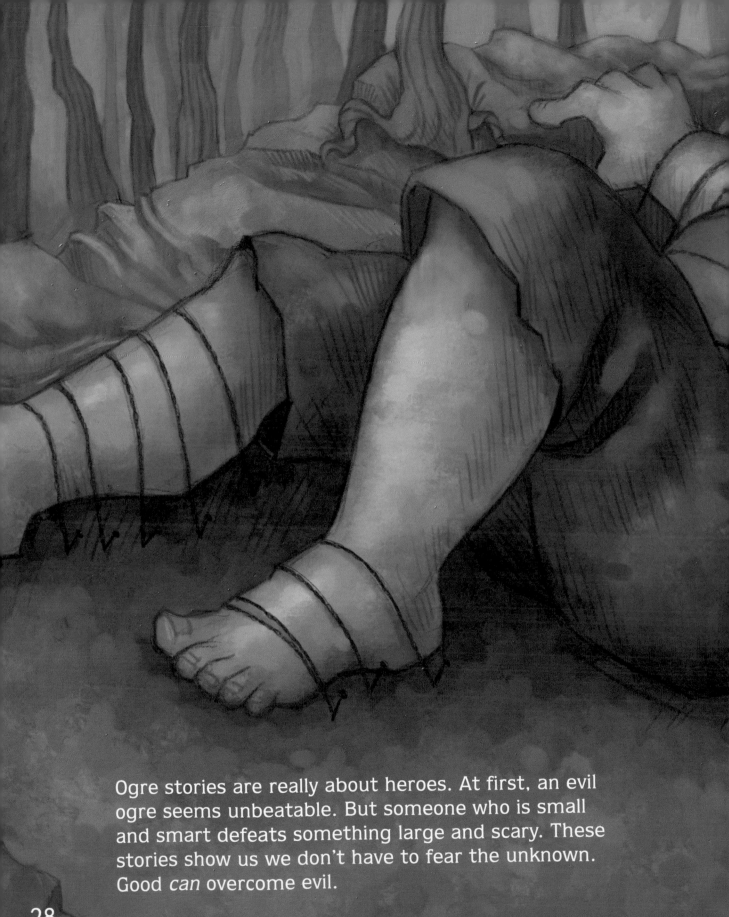

Ogre stories are really about heroes. At first, an evil ogre seems unbeatable. But someone who is small and smart defeats something large and scary. These stories show us we don't have to fear the unknown. Good *can* overcome evil.

Legend Has It

- Ogres are almost always evil. But in *The Good Ogre*, a kind ogre helps a man find money and a wife.

- Native Americans in northern Minnesota and Canada have passed down legends of a horrible ogre called the Wendigo. Some stories say that greedy people turn into Wendigos. A Wendigo roams the woods and loves to eat people.

- In Japanese legend, the *oni* is similar to an ogre. An oni is usually red, pink, or blue. It has horns and may have three eyes. It also has three fingers and three toes.

- In the *Shrek* movies, the ogre, Shrek, seems a bit grumpy. But he is actually a kind creature.

Glossary

author—a person who writes a book

defeat—to beat someone in a competition

dungeon—a strong underground prison cell in a castle

giant—a very large creature in fairy tales; usually shaped like a large human

greedy—selfishly wanting something, such as money or treasure

legend—a story that seems to be true and is handed down from earlier times

ogress—a female ogre

outsmart—to trick someone

Index

To Learn More

More Books to Read

Berk, Ari, Wayne Anderson, and Douglas Carrel. *The Secret History of Giants: Or Codex Giganticum.* Somerville, Mass.: Candelwick Press, 2008.

Cech, John, retold by. *Jack and the Beanstalk.* New York: Sterling Pub. Co., 2008.

Piumini, Roberto, retold by. *Puss in Boots.* Storybook Classics. Mankato, Minn.: Picture Window Books, 2010.

Steig, William. *Shrek!* New York: Farrar, Straus, Giroux, 1990.

Internet Sites

FactHound offers a safe, fun way to find Internet sites related to this book. All of the sites on FactHound have been researched by our staff.

Here's all you do:

Visit *www.facthound.com*

Type in this code: 9781404861596

Super-cool stuff!

Check out projects, games and lots more at **www.capstonekids.com**

Look for all the books in the Fairy-Tale Superstars series:

The Truth About Dragons

The Truth About Elves

The Truth About Fairies

The Truth About Ogres

The Truth About Princesses

The Truth About Trolls

The Truth About Unicorns

The Truth About Witches